AI Skills

YOUR PATH TO HIGH INCOME, IN-DEMAND SKILLS, AND FREEDOM

Written by

M. Aden

Table of Contents

The books you don't read, can't help you

CHAPTER 1

THE NEW ERA HAS BEGUN

We are standing at the edge of one of the greatest transformations in human history, a shift so powerful that it is changing the way we live, work, and dream. For centuries, technology has evolved slowly, machines replaced physical labor, computers replaced paper, and the internet connected us to the world. But nothing has accelerated change the way **artificial intelligence** has. AI is not just another invention; it is the beginning of a new era where knowledge, creativity, and opportunity are more accessible than ever before. This chapter is your doorway into that world. It will help you understand why AI matters, why now is the perfect time to learn it, and why ordinary people, people just like you, have more power, potential, and opportunity today than at any other point in human history.

To truly appreciate how significant this moment is, it helps to look back for a moment. Think about life before smartphones became part of our pockets. Think about how difficult communication used to be. Think about how limited online learning was before fast internet. Think about how impossible it would have seemed twenty years ago to work from home. Our world has been evolving, step by step, year after year. And at each stage, some people moved forward while others held back, unsure of the changes or afraid of trying something new. The same is happening now with AI.

Many people see it as something complicated, something meant only for experts or people in the tech world. But that is far from the truth. AI is not here to confuse or intimidate you. It is here to **help**, to support, to empower, and to make life easier. Once you understand this, everything changes.

AI has quietly been a part of your life for years, even if you didn't notice. When your phone corrects your spelling, that is AI. When YouTube recommends a video, that is AI. When Google maps out a faster route home, that is AI. When Netflix suggests a movie based on what you enjoy, that is AI. It has been around you, guiding small decisions, simplifying daily tasks, helping you operate more smoothly. But the difference today is that AI has become more interactive. Now, you can talk to it, collaborate with it, brainstorm ideas with it, plan your future with it, and use it to create things that once seemed impossible without years of training or experience.

This shift scares some people because it is new and fast. But fear is a natural reaction to change. Throughout history, every major technological breakthrough created fear. When electricity was introduced, people believed it was dangerous. When cars began replacing horses, many feared accidents and chaos. When computers first entered workplaces, people thought they would lose their jobs. But what happened instead? Every one of those inventions created more opportunities. They eliminated some old tasks, yes, but they created entire new industries, new roles, new ways of living, and new possibilities. AI is doing the same. It is not here to take everything away. It is here to open doors, if you are willing to walk through them.

You will hear people talk about AI replacing jobs, and while that fear is understandable, it is also incomplete. The truth is simple: ***AI will not replace people who learn how to use it. AI will replace people who refuse to adapt.*** Those who embrace AI will become faster, more creative, more productive, and more capable. Those who ignore it will find themselves struggling to keep up. But learning AI does not require special intelligence or a technical background. You do not need to understand programming or mathematics. What you need is curiosity and willingness. If you can type a sentence, you can learn how to use AI. If you can ask a question, you can generate ideas. If you can explain what you want, you can use AI to bring it to life. The entry barrier has never been lower.

Right now, from 2025 to 2030, the world is going through what many experts call the "AI opportunity window." It is a period when early learners, people who invest even a little bit of time into understanding AI, will gain huge advantages in careers, businesses, creativity, and personal growth. Think about the early days of YouTube, when ordinary creators uploaded simple videos and ended up building massive platforms. Think about the early influencers on Instagram who started with basic photos and later built entire businesses. Think about the first people who learned to build websites or run online stores, they earned more simply because they learned earlier. AI is the next version of that early opportunity. The people who learn it in these early years will shape the future. And you are right on time.

One of the most empowering truths about AI is that beginners have an advantage. People often think that being inexperienced makes learning AI harder, but it's the opposite. When you are new, you are flexible. You don't have old habits to unlearn. You don't overthink the process or fight against change. You experiment naturally. You explore freely. This makes you more adaptable to the new digital landscape. AI is a field where curiosity is more valuable than expertise. Every question you ask, every tool you try, every idea you test, these small actions add up and help you grow faster than you think.

AI is also equalizing the world in a way nothing else has. For generations, education and opportunities depended on income, geography, and access. People who couldn't afford expensive schools or professional training were often left behind. But today, AI gives you access to tools and knowledge that used to cost thousands of dollars or require years of study. You can write like a professional even if English is not your first language. You can design like an artist even if you've never taken a design class. You can generate business ideas even if you've never studied entrepreneurship. You can create videos, plan content, research topics, write books, and build digital products, all with AI guiding you step-by-step. It has removed the walls that once separated people. It has made success more reachable for anyone willing to learn.

Even with this massive opportunity, many people are still afraid. They believe they are "too late." They compare themselves to others who seem more confident or more experienced. They feel overwhelmed by new tools and worry that they won't understand them. But here is the truth: **you are not late. You are early.** Most people still don't know how to use AI well. Many are confused. Many haven't even opened ChatGPT or any other AI tool. Some think they will learn "next year" or "one day," but that day never comes. By starting now, you are placing yourself ahead of millions of others. You are choosing to be prepared instead of panicked. You are choosing to rise instead of resist. That choice alone separates you from the crowd.

Let me share a simple story that shows what is possible. A man named Daniel worked in a grocery store, stocking shelves every night. He felt exhausted and unfulfilled, living paycheck to paycheck. One evening, he heard someone mention AI writing tools. Curious, he went home and opened ChatGPT for the first time. He typed clumsily, unsure of what to say. But he kept trying. He asked AI to help him write descriptions for products. Then he used it to create small ads. Eventually, he built a simple portfolio. Within a few months, he started offering freelance writing services online. His first client paid him $50. Then another paid him $75. Gradually, his confidence grew. Within a year, he was earning more from freelancing than from his job. All because he took one small step, opening an AI tool.

Stories like Daniel's are happening everywhere. People with no background, no technical skills, no experience are changing their lives simply by learning how to work with AI. They are not geniuses. They are not privileged. They are not lucky. They simply started. That is what this book will help you do, start with clarity, confidence, and guidance, so you can unlock the opportunities awaiting you in this new age.

AI is not just a tool. It is a gateway to reinvention. It allows you to rethink your identity, rebuild your confidence, and rediscover your strengths. It allows you to dream bigger, act faster, and accomplish more. It allows you to become the version of yourself that you always believed you could be. You no longer have to wait years for success. You no longer have to feel limited by your circumstances. AI gives you the chance to grow into your potential with support, guidance, and powerful digital tools.

As you begin this journey, take a moment to reflect on what you truly want. What do you hope to create? What skills excite you? What fear do you want to let go of? What future do you want to build with AI at your side? Write down your own personal AI vision, a simple sentence that defines your direction, like:
"I will use AI to grow, learn, and create opportunities for my future."

This is your beginning. A new world is waiting, and you are stepping into it with courage. You are not late. You are exactly on time. And every page of this book will guide you toward a future filled with possibility.

When you're ready, let's continue.

Chapter 2

REWIRING YOUR MINDSET FOR AN AI-POWERED FUTURE

Stepping into the world of AI is not just about learning new tools; it is about reshaping the way you see yourself, your abilities, and your future. Technology can change quickly, but a strong, flexible mindset becomes the anchor that keeps you steady through every shift. Many people believe success in the digital age starts with technical knowledge, but the truth is that everything begins with your mind. Before you learn prompts, workflows, or AI tools, you must first build the internal foundation that allows you to adapt, grow, and thrive. This chapter is designed to help you shift your thinking, remove fears, and step into the world of AI with clarity, confidence, and purpose.

Fear vs. Opportunity, How the Mind Reacts to Change

Human beings naturally resist change. It is part of our biology. When something new emerges, like AI, the mind sends warnings: "What if I can't learn this?" "What if I'm too late?" "What if this replaces my job?" This fear is not a sign that you are weak or incapable; it is a sign that your brain is trying to protect you from the unfamiliar. But in moments of rapid technological growth, fear can become a barrier that blocks you from opportunities that are truly meant for you.

Every major transformation in history, from electricity to the internet, came with a wave of fear. People worried those changes would ruin everything. Instead, they created entirely new industries, careers, and possibilities. AI is no different. The fear you feel is a signal, but it does not have to be a limitation. You can choose to interpret fear as a message that you are standing at the edge of something important. When you shift your attention away from "What if this goes wrong?" to "What if this helps me succeed?", everything begins to change.

Fear shrinks your world; opportunity expands it. The difference between staying stuck and moving forward is not talent or intelligence, it is willingness. When you choose to see AI as the biggest tool of empowerment in the modern world rather than a threat, you position yourself for growth. You turn fear into fuel. The moment you start viewing AI as a partner, not an enemy, your relationship with the future transforms.

Leaving the Old Identity Behind

One of the hardest parts of adapting to a new era is letting go of old identities. Perhaps you see yourself as "not a tech person," "slow to learn," "too old to start," or "not smart enough for digital skills." These identities are not facts, they are stories you have repeated so many times that they feel true. But identities are flexible. You can rewrite them at any moment, especially when the world around you is evolving.

Holding on to old labels keeps you connected to an outdated version of yourself. The version of you who survives in the AI era is not the one clinging to who you used to be, it is the one who allows themselves to grow into someone new. Reinvention does not require you to forget the past; it only requires you to release the idea that you must stay the same. You are not supposed to repeat your old patterns, you are supposed to rise above them.

Letting go of an old identity is similar to clearing space in a room. Before you bring in something new, you must remove what is no longer useful. This means releasing the belief that technology is "too complicated," that learning is "too difficult," or that opportunities are "for younger people." When you wipe away these old mental labels, you give yourself permission to grow. You stop fighting with your potential and start embracing it. The new identity you build, confident, curious, capable, becomes the foundation for everything you create in the world of AI.

Developing a Growth-Mind Approach

A growth mindset means believing that you can learn, improve, and adapt through effort and consistency. This mindset is essential in the AI era because the world is changing too fast for fixed thinking. When you believe that your abilities are flexible, you allow yourself to become a learner again. You stop avoiding challenges and start embracing them as part of your evolution.

In a fixed mindset, mistakes feel like proof that you are not good enough. In a growth mindset, mistakes are simply data, information that shows you what to adjust next time. This approach removes the pressure to be perfect and replaces it with the freedom to explore. You begin to understand that mastery does not happen overnight. It builds slowly, through repeated effort, curiosity, and a willingness to experiment.

Developing a growth mindset also means being kind to yourself during the learning process. Instead of criticizing yourself for not understanding something immediately, you offer yourself patience and encouragement. You remind yourself that every expert was once a beginner. You speak to yourself in a way that inspires progress, not doubt. The more you practice this mindset, the easier it becomes to tackle new tools, new concepts, and new challenges without feeling overwhelmed.

Confidence Through Small Daily Actions

Confidence does not appear magically. It is built quietly, in the background, through consistent action. The small steps you take each day, spending ten minutes learning a new tool, practicing a prompt, exploring a feature, are what shape your belief in yourself. Every action tells your mind, "I can do this." And each time you push through discomfort, you strengthen that belief a little more.

People often think confidence comes from big achievements. But confidence truly comes from small wins. Completing your first prompt. Creating your first AI image. Writing your first idea. Building your first workflow. These little victories accumulate like bricks forming a strong foundation. When you recognize your progress, no matter how small, you reinforce your identity as someone capable of learning and growing.

Small daily actions also reduce overwhelm. Instead of trying to learn everything at once, which only triggers anxiety, you focus on manageable steps. Ten minutes here. Five minutes there. A small experiment today. A small improvement tomorrow. These actions compound over time and create powerful results. The more consistent you are, the easier learning becomes. And the easier learning becomes, the more confident you feel stepping into bigger opportunities.

Success Stories of Late Starters

One of the most beautiful truths about the AI revolution is that success is not limited to the young, the tech-savvy, or the academically gifted. Many people who started late, sometimes much later than they expected, have found new direction, new careers, and new confidence through AI.

There are individuals in their fifties and sixties who began experimenting with AI tools out of curiosity and ended up building small online businesses. People with no technology background have learned to create digital content, design graphics, write books, and even build websites with the support of AI. Stay-at-home parents, freelancers, retirees, teachers, and workers who felt "left behind" suddenly discovered that they were not behind at all, they simply needed the right tools and encouragement.

Late starters succeed because they bring something invaluable: life experience. While young people may learn faster, older learners often think deeper. They understand discipline, patience, responsibility, and commitment. AI tools simply amplify these qualities. They make it easier to turn an idea into a product, a skill into an income, or a dream into a reality.

The common thread in every late-starter success story is this: they gave themselves a chance. They stopped believing they were "too late" and realized they were right on time.

Staying Disciplined in a Distraction-Heavy World

We live in a world designed to pull your attention in every direction. Notifications, messages, endless scrolling, and constant noise make it hard to focus on learning. Discipline becomes more important than motivation. Motivation pushes you to start; discipline keeps you going even when the excitement fades.

To stay disciplined, you must create an environment that supports your goals. This may mean setting specific learning times, turning off distractions, dedicating a small workspace, or practicing a daily routine. The goal is not perfection, it is consistency. Even on days when you feel tired or discouraged, doing a small amount keeps your momentum alive.

Discipline is not about being strict; it is about being committed. You commit to your future self. You commit to growth. You commit to giving yourself the advantage you deserve. In a world full of distractions, being disciplined is a superpower. It ensures that you keep learning, keep improving, and keep moving forward, one day at a time.

Exercise: 5 Limiting Beliefs vs. 5 Empowered Beliefs

Take a moment to write down five limiting beliefs you currently hold about AI, learning, or your abilities. Then rewrite each one into an empowered belief. For example:

- *"I'm not good with technology" becomes "I can learn any tool one step at a time."*
- *"AI is too complicated for me" becomes "AI becomes easier every time I practice."*

This exercise helps retrain your mind and reshape your identity into someone who is capable, adaptable, and ready for the future.

Chapter 3

UNDERSTANDING AI IN THE SIMPLEST WAY POSSIBLE

Artificial Intelligence, or AI, is one of the most talked-about topics in the world today. It is reshaping industries, changing how people work, and opening doors to opportunities that seemed impossible just a few years ago. Yet, for many, AI remains a confusing, even intimidating concept. Some imagine it as robots taking over jobs, while others see it as a complicated, technical language only experts can understand. The truth is far simpler. AI is not magic, and it is not beyond your reach. In fact, understanding AI is easier than you think, and it starts with thinking of AI not as a machine, but as a tool that amplifies human intelligence.

The purpose of this chapter is to strip away the jargon, demystify the concepts, and show you that AI is something anyone can learn and use. By the end, you will not only understand what AI is and how it works, but you will also feel confident in using it to improve your life, work, and creativity.

What AI Actually Is, Human-Friendly Language

At its core, AI is simply a way for computers to perform tasks that normally require human intelligence. These tasks include understanding language, recognizing images, solving problems, and making decisions. Imagine teaching a computer to read a story and answer questions about it, or showing it thousands of pictures of cats so it can identify a cat in any new photo. That is AI in action.

Think of AI as a highly intelligent assistant. It can analyze large amounts of information quickly, recognize patterns you might miss, and provide suggestions to help you make decisions faster. AI does not think or feel like a human, but it can mimic certain aspects of human thinking to make our lives easier and more productive. It can write emails, create designs, summarize articles, generate ideas, and even compose music or create art. The key is that AI works *with* you, it amplifies your abilities rather than replacing them.

The beauty of AI is that it learns from data. Just as a child learns by observing, practicing, and receiving feedback, AI improves by analyzing information and making adjustments. The more it "sees" and "practices," the better it becomes at helping you. This makes it a tool that gets more powerful with use. The better you understand it, the more effectively you can apply it to your goals.

What AI Is NOT, Clearing Misconceptions

Before we dive deeper into AI, it's important to clear up some common misconceptions that often create fear or hesitation. First, AI is not sentient. It does not have emotions, consciousness, or intentions. It cannot decide to take over the world or form personal opinions. AI is a tool created and guided by humans, it only does what it is programmed or trained to do.

Second, AI is not an instant solution to every problem. It is not a magic wand that guarantees perfect results. AI works best when paired with human judgment, creativity, and critical thinking. It can suggest ideas, generate drafts, or automate repetitive tasks, but it cannot replace your ability to make thoughtful decisions or add personal insight.

Third, AI is not limited to computer programmers or technical experts. While some knowledge of programming can enhance what you do with AI, it is no longer a requirement. Modern AI tools are designed to be accessible to beginners. With simple prompts, clicks, and inputs, anyone can harness AI for productivity, learning, creativity, or business growth.

By understanding what AI is, and what it is not, you can approach it with clarity and confidence. This mindset reduces fear, encourages exploration, and empowers you to start using AI right now, even as a beginner.

Everyday AI Applications We Already Use

You may be surprised to learn that AI is already a part of daily life, often without us even noticing. Whenever you use a smartphone, AI is at work. Voice assistants like Siri, Alexa, or Google Assistant use AI to understand your commands and provide answers. Social media platforms employ AI to suggest content you might like, filter spam, and even recognize faces in photos. Email programs use AI to sort messages, flag important items, and suggest quick responses.

In banking, AI detects unusual transactions to prevent fraud. In healthcare, AI analyzes medical images to help doctors identify diseases earlier. Even online shopping relies on AI, suggesting products based on your browsing history and preferences. The key takeaway is that AI is not some distant, futuristic technology, it is already integrated into the tools and services you use every day. Understanding this can make AI feel more approachable and less intimidating.

Recognizing AI in everyday life also helps you see its potential in your personal and professional life. If it can recommend a movie or optimize an email workflow, imagine how it could help you brainstorm ideas, automate repetitive tasks, or create content quickly. The possibilities are limitless, and they start with simple understanding.

The Big AI Tools You Need to Know

While there are hundreds of AI tools, a few stand out for beginners because they are powerful, easy to use, and widely adopted. Some of the most well-known include:

ChatGPT: A conversational AI that can answer questions, generate content, write stories, and assist with problem-solving. It's like having a writing partner who never gets tired.

Claude: Similar to ChatGPT, Claude is designed to provide thoughtful responses to questions and tasks, often focusing on clarity and reasoning.

Gemini: A versatile AI that combines research, creative writing, and data analysis in one platform.

Midjourney: A tool for creating images and art from text prompts. It allows beginners and professionals to turn ideas into visuals without traditional design skills.

Perplexity: An AI tool focused on research and summarization, helping users quickly find and understand information.

These tools are not intimidating if you approach them with curiosity. You do not need to master them all at once. Start with one, experiment, and learn gradually. Over time, your familiarity with different tools will build confidence, allowing you to combine multiple AI applications for productivity and creativity.

The Rise of Automation

AI is a major driver of automation, which simply means using technology to handle repetitive or routine tasks. Automation can be as simple as automatically sorting emails or scheduling social media posts, or as complex as analyzing large datasets to make business predictions. The key benefit of automation is that it frees your time to focus on higher-value tasks, creativity, problem-solving, strategy, or personal growth.

Rather than seeing automation as a threat, think of it as an opportunity. The more mundane tasks AI can handle for you, the more energy you have to focus on what truly matters. This is why AI literacy is not optional, it is a critical skill for anyone who wants to remain productive, competitive, and relevant in a rapidly changing world.

Automation also helps beginners scale their efforts. Even without technical expertise, AI allows you to accomplish in hours what might have taken days or weeks manually. This creates confidence, efficiency, and a sense of control, even for those who have never used AI before.

Why AI Literacy Is the New Reading and Writing

In the 21st century, the ability to read, write, and communicate remains essential, but AI literacy is quickly becoming equally important. Understanding AI is no longer just for tech professionals, it is a fundamental skill for navigating daily life, work, and business. Just as reading opens doors to knowledge and opportunity, AI literacy opens doors to efficiency, creativity, and income.

Being AI literate does not mean you must memorize algorithms or write complex code. It means understanding what AI can and cannot do, knowing which tools to use, and learning how to interact with AI effectively. It is about using AI as a partner to enhance your thinking, productivity, and problem-solving skills. This literacy empowers you to make informed decisions, create smarter solutions, and confidently participate in the digital era.

By cultivating AI literacy, you are investing in yourself. You are preparing for opportunities that others may overlook. You are gaining the ability to experiment, innovate, and compete in ways that were previously unimaginable. In many ways, AI literacy is the bridge between your current abilities and your future potential.

Exercise: Explain AI in Your Own Words

Now that you understand the basics, take a moment to write your own definition of AI. Don't worry about getting it perfect. The goal is to put your understanding into words, which helps solidify your knowledge. For example, you might write something like:

"AI is a tool that helps me do tasks faster, analyze information, and create new ideas, working as my intelligent assistant."

After writing your definition, consider answering these questions:

- What tasks could AI help me with today?
- Which AI tool am I most interested in exploring first?
- How could learning AI change my work, learning, or daily life?

This exercise is more than a reflection, it is the first step in making AI a practical and powerful part of your life. Writing it down transforms abstract concepts into actionable understanding, giving you a foundation for experimenting, learning, and growing with AI.

Final Thoughts

Understanding AI may seem intimidating at first, but it doesn't have to be. By thinking of AI in human-friendly terms, clearing misconceptions, recognizing its everyday applications, exploring key tools, and appreciating the rise of automation, you have taken the first step toward mastery. AI is not a distant or threatening force, it is a practical, accessible tool that can enhance your skills, creativity, and income.

The journey of AI learning begins with curiosity and confidence. Remember, the goal is not to become an expert overnight but to start using AI in small, consistent ways that improve your life. Every prompt, every experiment, every new skill builds your understanding and strengthens your digital literacy. The more you practice, the more AI becomes a trusted partner, helping you achieve goals faster and more creatively than you could alone.

As you continue on this journey, hold onto the mindset that you are capable of learning and adapting. The tools exist, the opportunities are real, and your willingness to explore will define your success. Understanding AI is not just about technology, it is about empowerment, confidence, and stepping into a future where you control your growth, creativity, and potential.

By the end of this chapter, you are no longer just a reader, you are a beginner practitioner of AI, ready to explore, experiment, and take action. And as you move forward, remember: the more familiar AI becomes, the more it transforms from a mysterious concept into a powerful partner in building the life, skills, and income you desire.

Chapter 4

The Essential AI Skills Every Beginner Must Learn

Entering the world of AI can feel overwhelming at first. There are countless tools, platforms, and applications, and it is easy to wonder where to start. The key to success, however, is not trying to learn everything at once, it is focusing on the essential skills that give you the ability to navigate, create, and leverage AI in your daily life and work. These foundational skills act as a springboard, helping you gain confidence, develop practical abilities, and start producing results quickly. By mastering these core skills, you are not only preparing for today's opportunities but also building resilience for the rapidly changing future.

This chapter is designed to help beginners understand which skills matter most, why they matter, and how to start practicing them immediately. Each skill is explained in simple, practical terms, with examples and exercises to make learning actionable. By the end, you will have a clear roadmap for building AI proficiency from the ground up.

AI Prompting Basics, Communicating Effectively with AI

At the heart of AI use is a skill called prompting. Prompting is simply giving instructions to AI in a way that it can understand and respond effectively. Think of it like asking a question or giving directions to an assistant, you need to be clear, specific, and intentional.

For beginners, the first step is learning to write prompts that are simple but precise. Instead of typing, "Write something about business," you might say, "Write a 300-word blog post about how small businesses can use AI for social media marketing, including examples and tips for beginners." The second prompt is far more actionable for AI.

Prompting is a skill you can improve through practice. Start by experimenting with small, simple prompts. Notice how slight changes in wording affect the output. Over time, you will develop a sense of how to communicate with AI in ways that produce high-quality results consistently.

Prompting is not only about technical skill; it is about thinking critically. You learn to structure your questions, anticipate outcomes, and refine your requests. Every prompt you write strengthens your ability to think, communicate, and solve problems in the AI era.

How to Talk to AI Like a Partner

Once you understand prompting, the next step is treating AI as a collaborative partner. AI is not just a tool you command, it is a creative assistant that can amplify your thinking. When you approach AI as a partner, you begin to experiment, brainstorm, and explore new ideas more effectively.

For example, instead of asking AI to "Write a story," you can start a conversation: "I want to create a story for children about a brave star named Luma who travels to different planets. Can you help me brainstorm three plot ideas, each with a lesson about courage?" Here, AI is not replacing your creativity, it is enhancing it. You remain the author, the guide, and the decision-maker.

Treating AI as a partner also means iterating. You ask questions, receive suggestions, refine, and try again. Collaboration with AI is an active process, not a passive one. This mindset shift, from seeing AI as a replacement to seeing it as a partner, is critical for beginners who want to move from experimentation to mastery.

Brainstorming with AI

One of the most powerful skills AI offers is the ability to brainstorm ideas rapidly. Whether you are writing content, planning a project, creating designs, or starting a business, AI can help you generate hundreds of ideas in minutes.

For example, suppose you want to start an online business. You could ask AI, "Give me 20 ideas for digital products I can sell online, suitable for beginners with no technical skills." AI will provide a list of options, and from there, you can choose, combine, or refine ideas. What would normally take hours or days can now be done in minutes.

Brainstorming with AI is not about copying suggestions blindly, it is about expanding your thinking. You can take AI's output as a starting point, adjust it, and apply your own creativity. Over time, this process trains your brain to think bigger, explore new perspectives, and make connections that you might have missed on your own.

Research with AI

Research is another essential AI skill. Whether you are learning a new topic, writing an article, or analyzing a market, AI can help you find, summarize, and organize information faster than traditional methods.

AI research can include summarizing articles, extracting key points from long documents, and comparing multiple sources of information. For beginners, start by asking AI to summarize a topic in simple language. For instance, "Explain blockchain technology in plain English for beginners." You can then dig deeper into the points that interest you most.

The value of AI in research is not only speed but also clarity. Instead of being overwhelmed by massive amounts of information online, AI helps you focus on what is important, digest knowledge quickly, and make informed decisions. This skill becomes especially useful in professional or creative work, where understanding a subject thoroughly and efficiently can give you a competitive advantage.

Writing and Editing

Writing is one of the most practical and high-value skills you can develop with AI. AI can help with everything from drafting emails and blog posts to creating books, scripts, or marketing copy. For beginners, the key is to use AI as a first draft partner rather than a final author.

Start by generating content quickly. For example, you might ask AI, "Write a 500-word article about the benefits of meditation for beginners, including practical tips." Once AI produces a draft, review it, edit it, and add your voice. You remain the author; AI is simply helping you get started and overcome writer's block.

Editing with AI is equally valuable. You can ask it to simplify sentences, check grammar, improve tone, or reformat text for clarity. By combining AI drafting and editing, you can produce polished content faster than ever before. This skill is especially powerful for anyone who wants to create content professionally, start a blog, or communicate more effectively in the digital age.

Productivity Workflows

AI is also a game-changer for productivity. Learning how to use AI to automate tasks, organize your day, and streamline workflows can free up hours each week. For example, AI can help you schedule meetings, draft standard responses, summarize notes, or track tasks.

Beginners can start small: identify one repetitive task in their daily routine and ask AI to help automate it. For instance, "Create a weekly social media posting schedule for my Instagram page," or "Summarize this week's emails and highlight important action items." Small improvements accumulate into significant time savings, allowing you to focus on higher-value activities like learning new skills or creating content.

Learning AI-powered productivity also trains you to think systemically. You begin to see tasks as processes that can be optimized, automated, or delegated. This mindset is invaluable in a world where efficiency and creativity are increasingly intertwined.

Automation Basics

Automation is one of the most exciting areas of AI because it allows you to do more with less effort. Even beginners can learn the basics of automation without coding or advanced technical knowledge.

Start by thinking of a task you do repeatedly, such as sending newsletters, posting on social media, or generating reports. Then ask AI to help you create a system that handles parts of that task automatically. Many AI platforms now provide simple drag-and-drop interfaces or step-by-step prompts for automation.

Understanding automation is not just about saving time, it is about creating leverage. With the right automated workflows, you can accomplish tasks that previously took hours in minutes, and scale your efforts without adding stress. Over time, these skills make you more productive, creative, and confident in navigating the AI-powered future.

Practical Exercise: Create Your First AI Workflow

To put these skills into practice, choose a small task you do regularly and design a simple AI workflow. For example:

1. Identify a repetitive task (e.g., writing a weekly social media post).
2. Ask AI to generate ideas or drafts for the task.
3. Edit or customize AI's output.
4. Schedule or automate delivery if possible.
5. Track time saved and note improvements.

By completing this exercise, you begin to understand how AI can integrate into your daily life, making your work faster, easier, and more efficient. This exercise also builds confidence, showing that AI is not complicated, it is a practical partner for solving real problems.

Building Confidence Through Practice

The skills outlined in this chapter, prompting, collaborative AI use, brainstorming, research, writing, productivity, and automation, are the foundation of everything you will do with AI. Mastering them takes time, but progress happens quickly when you practice consistently. Focus on small, manageable steps. Each prompt, each workflow, and each completed task reinforces your competence. Confidence is built not by knowing everything, but by acting consistently, learning from experience, and celebrating small wins along the way.

Remember, mastery of AI is not about speed, it is about understanding, applying, and growing. Every small skill learned today becomes a building block for bigger achievements tomorrow. Over time, these foundational skills compound, turning beginners into confident users who can leverage AI to create content, streamline work, and explore new opportunities.

Final Thoughts

AI can seem complex, but at its core, it is a set of skills that anyone can learn. By focusing on essential skills, prompting, collaboration, brainstorming, research, writing, productivity, and automation, you establish a foundation that allows you to grow quickly and effectively. These skills are practical, high-value, and immediately applicable, giving you tangible results while building your confidence.

The journey of AI mastery begins with understanding, followed by practice and experimentation. Each small step you take expands your ability to navigate the AI landscape, create with purpose, and use technology to achieve your goals. By investing time in these essential skills now, you are not just learning tools, you are building a mindset, a workflow, and a foundation for lifelong success in an AI-powered world.

Start small, stay consistent, and remember: the essential skills you build today will carry you into tomorrow's opportunities. With each new skill, you become more capable, more confident, and more prepared to take advantage of the digital era. The AI future is not intimidating, it is a space of endless possibility, waiting for you to step in and claim it.

CHAPTER 5

HIGH-INCOME DIGITAL SKILLS YOU CAN LEARN WITH AI

The digital world has changed dramatically, and with AI advancing so quickly, the skills that once took years to master can now be learned in months, sometimes even weeks. This chapter is designed to open your mind to what is truly possible for you. You are no longer limited by your background, your age, your location, or the opportunities around you. What matters now is your willingness to learn, experiment, and build. AI has leveled the playing field in a way humanity has never seen before.

The most powerful thing to understand is this: **high-income skills are no longer only for "experts."**

AI acts like a partner that helps you think faster, create better, and work smarter. Whether you are a student, a stay-at-home parent, an employee, or someone who has struggled to start fresh, AI gives you the chance to step into a world where your creativity becomes currency and your ideas turn into income.

This chapter will guide you through the most profitable digital skills that AI can help you learn, not in five years, not in 500 hours of training, but in a way that is realistic, learnable, and achievable for you. These skills are already changing lives around the world, and by the end of this chapter, you will know exactly which one you want to focus on.

AI Writing + Content Creation

Writing used to be something people believed only authors, journalists, or "talented creatives" could do. Today, AI has transformed writing into a skill anyone can master. Whether you want to create content for social media, write blog posts, create e-books, or even sell your writing services, AI becomes your creative partner. It doesn't replace your voice; it enhances it.

You can brainstorm ideas effortlessly, generate storylines, write product descriptions, create marketing messages, or draft outlines for any type of content. When you combine AI with your unique perspective, personality, and story, you become unstoppable. Many people are now earning through freelance writing, brand storytelling, and content production simply by mastering how to collaborate with tools like ChatGPT, Claude, or Gemini.

AI also helps you learn structure. If you've ever felt lost staring at a blank page, AI removes that fear. You can ask it: "Give me the structure of a blog post," or "Help me improve my paragraph," and within seconds, you are flowing. Over time, your writing improves naturally. Clients don't care whether you used AI, they care about results. And with AI, you can deliver fast, clear, high-quality writing that stands out.

AI Social Media Management

We live in a world where businesses grow online before they grow anywhere else. This has made social media management one of the most profitable skills, especially now that AI amplifies what one person can do. Instead of spending hours planning posts, editing captions, or researching trends, AI tools can do the heavy lifting while you focus on creativity and engagement.

Social media is not just posting pretty pictures anymore. It is about strategy, understanding people, and creating content that feels human and relatable. With AI, you can generate monthly content calendars, analyze audience behavior, and create engaging captions in seconds. You can understand what type of content performs best on platforms like Instagram, TikTok, YouTube, or Facebook.

This skill has become so powerful that many freelancers earn full-time income managing one or two clients. AI helps you automate tasks, monitor performance, and stay consistent without burning out. If you enjoy storytelling, communication, or visual creativity, social media management is one of the easiest high-income skills to start with, because AI does 40–60% of the groundwork for you.

AI Video Creation

Video is the king of modern content. More people watch videos than read posts, and businesses know that video marketing increases sales dramatically. The best part? You no longer need a camera, expensive equipment, or advanced editing skills. AI tools can help you create professional-quality videos using text, voice, and simple drag-and-drop editors.

Tools like Runway, HeyGen, Pika Labs, and Descript can turn simple ideas into videos with animations, transitions, subtitles, and effects. This skill is especially profitable because video editing used to be complex, time-consuming, and difficult to learn. Now, AI handles the hardest steps while you guide the creative direction.

People who learn AI video creation are landing powerful opportunities, from creating YouTube videos and brand ads to producing short-form content for businesses. If you enjoy visuals, storytelling, or media, video creation can quickly become your most valuable skill. And because AI speeds up everything, you can produce more content in less time, making you a highly desirable creator in today's world.

AI Graphic Design

Graphic design is no longer limited to people who went to art school or mastered Adobe Photoshop. AI design tools like Midjourney, Canva AI, and Adobe

Firefly can generate stunning designs, illustrations, logos, posters, and brand assets in minutes.

What makes AI design so powerful is the freedom it gives beginners. You don't need to draw. You don't need to understand color theory. You don't need to know advanced design principles from day one. AI teaches you while helping you create. As you experiment, your understanding naturally grows.

Design is one of the highest-demand services online, and with AI, you can offer work that looks advanced, clean, and professional. From children's book illustrations to social media graphics, business branding, invitations, and product packaging, the possibilities are endless. The more you practice prompts and refine your style, the better your results become, and the more value you can offer.

AI Coding Assistance

This is one of the biggest breakthroughs of our generation. For decades, coding was seen as one of the hardest skills someone could learn. Today, AI tools like GitHub Copilot, ChatGPT, and Replit give anyone the ability to create websites, apps, automations, and digital tools, even if they have never coded before.

AI explains code step-by-step. It gives examples. It identifies errors. It corrects your mistakes. It helps you build real solutions by guiding you through the process. This doesn't mean every beginner becomes a "software engineer," but it does mean you can automate tasks, build digital products, and solve problems for clients in ways that were impossible before.

The ability to understand even basic coding concepts opens doors. It helps you become more competitive in the job market. It allows you to create your own tools that make your work faster and easier. And with AI handling most of the logical work, you can focus on learning the parts you enjoy most.

AI Research and Analysis

Information is power, and we live in the information age. AI gives you instant access to research that used to take hours or days. You can analyze trends, summarize long documents, study industries, explore new markets, read competitors, and extract insights in minutes.

This skill is especially valuable in business, e-commerce, writing, marketing, and consulting. Companies pay for clarity. They pay for people who can make sense of data. They pay for people who can take information and turn it into action. AI helps you develop this ability even if you've never done formal research before.

Whether you want to start a business, create digital products, or help other companies grow, research and analysis will always be a profitable skill. With AI, it becomes faster, deeper, and more accessible than ever.

Building a Personal Brand with AI

In today's world, people don't just buy products, they buy personalities, voices, and trust. A personal brand is simply your digital identity: what you stand for, your story, your message, and the value you give to others. AI helps you build a brand even if you don't know how to start.

You can create consistent content, design your online presence, write your bio, develop your message, and build a community with the help of AI tools. You don't need to be famous. You don't need to be an expert. You just need to show up, share value, and be yourself. AI supports the strategy so you can focus on authenticity.

Building a brand is one of the most long-term, profitable things you can do. It opens doors to income, partnerships, opportunities, and growth. With AI, you can build it faster and smarter than ever before.

Exercise: Choose ONE Skill to Focus on This Week

Do not overwhelm yourself by trying to master everything at once. Growth comes from focus. Choose one of the skills from this chapter, the one that made your heart feel excited or curious, and dedicate this week to exploring it. Not to become an expert, but to begin. To practice. To learn. To experiment.

AI has already given you the tools. Now you must give yourself the permission to start.

CHAPTER 6

HOW TO USE AI TO EARN MONEY (BEGINNER TO PRO)

For years, earning money online was seen as something mysterious, complicated, or reserved for people who were already successful. Many felt they didn't have the skills, confidence, or opportunity to start. But this era is different. AI has shifted the landscape so dramatically that people from every age, education level, and background are earning income online, not because they are experts, but because they learned how to use smart tools. You no longer need decades of experience or fancy equipment. What you need now is curiosity, consistency, and the willingness to try.

This chapter is your roadmap. It strips away confusion and shows you clear income paths you can start even if you consider yourself a complete beginner. Nothing here is theory. These are real methods that people are using every day to earn anywhere from a few hundred dollars a month to full-time income. Some do it part-time. Some do it after work. Some turn it into a business. What matters most is understanding that **earning with AI is not about replacing humans, it's about enhancing what humans can do.**

AI multiplies your creativity. It sharpens your ideas. It speeds up your work. It gives you the ability to deliver results that look professional even if you are just starting out. And the best part? AI gives you a level of confidence you may have never felt before because you always have support, guidance, and creative direction at your fingertips.

In this chapter, we explore the most realistic ways to earn money with AI, from freelancing to digital products, micro-agencies, consulting, selling prompts, and more. You will also read inspiring case studies of ordinary people who turned small opportunities into meaningful income. By the end, you will have a clear idea of how *you* want to begin, and the confidence to take that first step.

Freelancing With AI

Freelancing is one of the fastest and most accessible ways to make money using AI because it does not require starting a business or building an audience. All you need is a skill, and AI helps you develop that skill quickly. Platforms like Upwork, Fiverr, Freelancer, and even social media communities are filled with clients looking for writing, content creation, research, design, video editing, marketing, and virtual assistance.

AI becomes your behind-the-scenes partner. If you are a writer, AI helps you plan, structure, and improve. If you are a designer, AI enhances creativity and helps you generate concepts. If you create videos, AI edits, writes scripts, or adds automation. Even tasks like emails, spreadsheets, and administration become easier with AI assistance.

Many new freelancers use AI to offer services such as:

- Writing content for blogs and websites.
- Designing social media posts and brand kits.
- Editing videos and creating promotional content.
- Researching and summarizing market trends.
- Managing social media accounts.
- creating resumes, presentations, and reports.

The key is not to sell "AI services" but to sell the **results** clients want. They do not care how you create the work. They care that it is fast, high quality, and effective.

Freelancing also helps you learn how to work with clients, understand deadlines, and build confidence.

The more you practice, the more you grow. With AI, you can deliver at a speed and quality that used to take years to develop, and that gives you a powerful advantage.

Selling Digital Products

Digital products are one of the most lucrative AI-powered income models because you create something once and sell it repeatedly without extra work. They don't require shipping, inventory, or large investment. AI helps you create high-quality digital products faster than ever.

Some of the most popular digital products include eBooks, templates, planners, guides, children's books, printable activities, business resources, social media kits, and courses. AI tools like ChatGPT, Midjourney, Canva, and Notion make it possible to design beautiful, useful products in a short time.

People love digital products because they solve problems. A fitness planner helps someone get organized. A budgeting template helps someone manage their money. A children's storybook entertains and educates. With AI, you can create designs, write content, structure the product, and even generate promotional materials.

Platforms like Etsy, Gumroad, Shopify, Payhip, and Amazon KDP allow you to list your products for global audiences. The more high-quality products you create, the more your income grows. This model works incredibly well for beginners because it does not require direct client work, making it a perfect option for people who prefer independence.

AI Side Hustles

Side hustles are the bridge between learning and earning, small projects that allow you to test ideas, experiment, and build confidence without pressure.

AI opens the door to a wide range of side hustles that require creativity more than expertise.

One of the most common side hustles is creating short-form content for brands and influencers. With AI writing scripts, generating ideas, and designing visuals, you can deliver high-quality results quickly. Another powerful side hustle is proofreading or editing, AI helps clean up grammar, fix structure, and simplify the process.

Some people start by offering research support, such as summarizing documents or conducting competitor analysis. Others provide email management, virtual assistance, or social media caption writing. AI tools streamline these tasks, allowing you to earn a flexible income with minimal stress.

The beauty of AI side hustles is that they fit into your lifestyle. You can do them after work, during weekends, or even while studying. They also help you discover what skills you enjoy most, which is useful when you want to scale into something bigger later.

Starting a Micro-Agency

If you enjoy working with clients and want a more structured income model, starting a micro-agency is a powerful next step. A micro-agency is simply a very small digital services company, often managed by one person using AI tools to amplify productivity.

You might offer services such as marketing, content creation, design, branding, automation, or video production. With AI as your co-worker, you can manage multiple clients without feeling overwhelmed. You don't need employees at the beginning because AI handles tasks like writing, editing, brainstorming, scheduling, and research.

What makes micro-agencies profitable is that clients often prefer working with small teams. Agencies feel personal, flexible, and efficient. And because AI saves you hours of manual work, your profit margins become higher. Over time, you can expand by hiring freelancers, building systems, or specializing in niches like real estate marketing, restaurant branding, or children's book publishing support.

A micro-agency is perfect if you want more control over your schedule and income while still enjoying the structure of client work.

Selling Prompts

Prompt selling is one of the newest and most creative income streams in the AI world. Prompts are simply instructions that tell AI what to create. A well-crafted prompt can generate stunning art, perfect writing, detailed research, or advanced automation. People buy prompts because they want fast results without learning how to write them.

For example, digital artists create prompt packs for Midjourney or DALL·E. Writers create prompt templates for story outlines or business emails. Designers create prompts that generate branded visuals. Educators create prompt kits for lesson planning, worksheets, or coaching.

Platforms like PromptBase and Etsy allow creators to sell their prompt collections, while others sell them directly on social media. It's a low-effort, high-creativity side hustle that can grow into steady income once you understand how to build effective prompts.

What makes this income stream so accessible is that prompts require imagination more than technical skill. If you enjoy experimenting with AI, this could become one of your easiest ways to earn.

Consulting With AI

Consulting is not just for experts, it is for anyone who can solve a problem. AI makes you smarter, faster, and more prepared, allowing you to offer valuable guidance even as a beginner. Many people underestimate how much they already know. For example, if you understand how to use social media, create content with AI, design branding, build digital products, or manage online tools, you already have consulting value.

Businesses often need help understanding how to use AI to improve their marketing, save time, automate tasks, or increase revenue. They want to know how to write prompts, create workflows, and integrate AI into their daily operations. You can offer one-on-one sessions, create guides, or develop AI strategies for small businesses.

Consulting is powerful because it positions you as someone who brings clarity in a confusing world. And with AI tools assisting you with research, planning, and execution, you can deliver high-quality insights that help clients feel confident and supported.

Case Studies: Real People Earning $500–$10,000 Per Month

Stories change belief. When you read about people who succeeded, you begin to understand that it is possible for you too. These case studies highlight real examples of individuals earning with AI, not because they were brilliant, but because they started.

One example is a college student who used ChatGPT to offer writing services on Fiverr. She began by charging small amounts for blog posts and social media captions. Over time, AI helped her improve her quality and speed. Now she consistently earns around $800–$1,200 per month while studying full-time.

Another example is a stay-at-home father who used Midjourney and Canva to design children's book illustrations. He began creating simple books for Amazon KDP and printable activity packs for Etsy. Today he makes between $2,000–$3,000 per month passively from digital products.

A third story comes from a corporate employee who was burnt out and looking for financial freedom. She started offering social media management using AI tools to automate scheduling and content creation. Within six months, she grew her client base to five businesses, earning around $4,000 per month with part-time effort.

Finally, a freelance marketer built a micro-agency offering AI-powered video ads for local businesses. With AI tools, he produced content that looked polished and professional. Some months he earns $8,000–$10,000 depending on client load. What started as a small side project became a thriving career.

These stories show that AI is not about luck; it is about taking advantage of opportunity and being willing to begin.

Exercise: Create Your First AI Income Plan

Take a moment to reflect. Out of all the income streams in this chapter, freelancing, digital products, side hustles, micro-agencies, prompt selling, or consulting, which one felt the most exciting? Which one made you curious? Which one felt achievable?

Your exercise is simple:

Choose one income path and write a one-week plan.

Not a perfect plan, just a starting plan.

Write down what you will learn, what you will create, and what your first step will be.

Your future begins not with a giant leap but with a small, confident decision.

CHAPTER 7

MASTERING AI TOOLS: A BEGINNER'S ROADMAP

Entering the world of AI tools can feel like standing in front of a huge buffet with a thousand options. It's tempting to try everything, but that approach quickly leads to overwhelm and confusion. The smarter way is to focus on a handful of reliable, beginner-friendly tools that cover the jobs you care about, writing, design, video, and productivity, and then practice them deliberately, a little each day.

This chapter gives you a practical roadmap: which tools to start with, why they matter, how to practice them in just 20 minutes a day, and how to avoid the common traps that derail beginners. By the end you'll have a simple daily system you can use immediately to build skill, confidence, and usable work you can show to others.

Start Small: Why Tool Choice Matters More Than Quantity

Before we jump into specific tools, let's clarify an important idea: it's better to know a few tools really well than to dabble in many tools poorly. Each tool has its strengths and quirks. When you learn the logic and workflow of one writing tool, one design tool, and one productivity tool, you'll find it easy to transfer those habits to others. Start by choosing one tool for each category you care about, learn it until it feels comfortable, and then add more once you have a routine. This focused approach reduces noise, speeds up progress, and builds the muscle memory you need to move from beginner to independent creator.

AI Writing Tools, ChatGPT, Claude, and How to Use Them

AI writing tools are the most direct way to get results fast. At the simplest level, they turn a few lines of instruction into drafts, outlines, emails, social posts, and even book chapters. ChatGPT and Claude are two of the most popular examples; they behave like conversational writing partners. The basic workflow is the same: give the AI context, ask for a clear deliverable, then iterate and refine. For example, instead of "write an email," say, "Write a friendly 150-word welcome email to new subscribers for a parenting newsletter, include a 1-sentence prompt to encourage reply." The clearer your input, the better the output.

To master these tools, practice three habits. First, learn to craft clear prompts: include audience, tone, length, and purpose. Second, use the tool's revision features, ask it to shorten, expand, list benefits, or change tone.

Third, always edit the output to inject your voice and verify facts. Over time you'll develop a mental checklist for prompts that consistently produce strong first drafts. That checklist will save you hours and produce work that looks professional quickly.

AI Design Tools, Canva, Midjourney, and the Designer's Workflow

Design used to require expensive software and long learning curves. Today, tools like Canva provide drag-and-drop simplicity plus AI features for layouts, color palettes, and text generation, while image-generation tools such as Midjourney let you create unique visuals from simple text prompts. The practical approach is to use Canva for layout and multipage projects (presentations, social posts, ebooks) and a generative image tool for hero images, concept art, or imaginative illustrations.

The core skill is learning to translate your idea into a design brief. Begin with a one-sentence description of what you want, then add specifics about colors, mood, and any text. For example: “Create a playful book cover for a children’s story about a brave frog learning to swim; bright colors, friendly font, smiling frog in water.” Feed that brief to a generative image tool for hero art, then import the image into Canva for typography, layout, and exporting in the right sizes. Practice composing briefs, tweaking results, and combining image generation with layout work until the process becomes second nature.

AI Video Tools, Runway, Pika, and Fast Visual Storytelling

Video is the most compelling content format today, and AI has made video creation far more accessible. Tools like Runway and Pika simplify editing, convert text to video, create captions automatically, and can even assist with background removal or voiceovers. The workflow to learn is straightforward: script → visuals → edit → refine. Start by writing short scripts with your writing AI (one to three sentences per scene), then let a video AI help you stitch stock clips, images, or generated visuals into a short clip. Use automated captioning and trimming tools to optimize pacing for platforms like Instagram or TikTok.

Practice pacing by focusing on very short formats first, 30 to 60 seconds. This constraint forces clarity and helps you learn editing rhythm quickly. Learn to use jump cuts, title cards, and B-roll to keep attention. Most beginners are surprised how quickly they can produce a shareable video once they have a repeatable script-to-publish workflow. Keep the bar low at first: a 30-second video published weekly is far better for learning than waiting to create a long, perfect video.

AI Productivity Tools, Notion AI, Zapier AI, and System Thinking

Creating and managing work is as important as creating content. Productivity tools like Notion AI and automation services like Zapier AI help you build systems that reduce busywork. Notion AI can summarize meeting notes, generate task lists from an idea, or help you draft project plans. Zapier AI connects apps, automating repetitive flows like saving form responses to a spreadsheet and notifying you in chat. Together, they allow you to scale simple projects without adding hours of manual work.

To get comfortable, map one workflow you repeat frequently, like content planning or client onboarding, and rebuild it using Notion and a single Zapier automation. The skill to learn is systems thinking: break down a process into steps, identify repetitive parts, then delegate those to AI. Once you do this a few times, you'll see compound time savings. Productivity mastery is the quiet superpower that allows you to produce more with less effort.

How to Practice 20 Minutes a Day, Consistency Over Intensity

A daily practice habit of 20 minutes is one of the most powerful strategies for mastering AI tools. Short, focused sessions beat long, irregular bursts because they build momentum and avoid burnout. Structure your 20 minutes like this: five minutes to plan (what you'll try), ten minutes to practice (writing prompts, designing, editing), and five minutes to reflect and save what you learned. Reflection is the secret ingredient, note what worked, which prompts produced the best output, and what you'd change tomorrow.

Rotate tool focus across the week. For example, Monday and Thursday for writing tools, Tuesday for design, Wednesday for video, and Friday for productivity automations. This rotation gives you consistent exposure without overwhelming one day. When you have only 20 minutes, prioritize doing an entire micro-task from start to finish, draft a short post, generate an image and put it into a layout, or automate one step in a workflow. Completing the micro-task delivers a sense of progress and keeps the practice habit alive.

How to Avoid Overwhelm, Simple Rules to Stay Sane

Overwhelm usually comes from two sources: trying too many tools and chasing perfection. Create simple rules to protect your energy. First, limit tool exploration to one new app per month. Second, set a "publish over polish" rule, get things out into the world even if they're not perfect. Third, create an "idea inbox" where wild ideas live while your daily practice focuses on the plan at hand. Finally, use timeboxing: give yourself 20 minutes and stop when the timer ends. These rules keep learning sustainable and prevent the common cycle of hopping between shiny tools without building lasting skill.

Another practical tip is to curate an essential toolkit. Think "pocket tools" that meet 80% of your needs: one writing AI, one image generator, one design/layout app, and one automation tool. When you master these, you'll find that many other tools feel like small variations of what you already know, making future learning faster and less stressful.

From Beginner to Confident User, A Sample 12-Week Roadmap

A short roadmap helps turn vague goals into clear action. Here's a simple 12-week path you can follow. In Weeks 1–4, focus on one writing tool: learn prompt structure, draft five pieces, and revise them. Weeks 5–8 pick a design tool: generate images, make three layouts, and export them for social or print. Weeks 9–10 move into short video: write scripts, make two 60-second videos, and publish them. Weeks 11–12 build a productivity automation that supports these outputs, automate social scheduling or collect feedback automatically. Each four-week block builds a usable output you can show and iterate on. The point is progress, not perfection; this rhythm ensures you finish projects and collect real results.

Practice Tools and Templates, Small Habits, Big Impact

Create a small notebook or a digital doc where you keep your best prompts, favorite templates, and lessons learned. When a prompt works well, save it. When a layout hits a good ratio of image-to-text, record it. Over three months, you'll compile a personal library that dramatically speeds up future work. Think of these templates as your training wheels; they reduce friction and let you move faster while learning.

Another tiny but powerful habit is sharing what you created. Post one small thing publicly each week. This forces completion, builds confidence, and creates momentum. It also builds an informal portfolio you can show to clients or collaborators.

Exercise: Build Your Daily 20-Minute AI Practice System

Now it's time to create your own practice system. Use this template and customize it.

1. Choose your four core tools, one for writing, one for design, one for video, one for productivity.
2. Block 20 minutes in your calendar each weekday.
3. Week A schedule example: Monday (writing), Tuesday (design), Wednesday (video), Thursday (productivity), Friday (revisit/portfolio).
4. Each session: 5 minutes plan, 10 minutes practice, 5 minutes reflect/save.
5. At the end of each week, pick one micro-output to publish: a social post, a single-page PDF, a short clip, or an automated task completed.

Commit to this system for 30 days. Track your progress in small notes, what worked, what didn't, and one thing you'll tweak next week. By the end of the month you'll have at least five concrete outputs, a small library of prompts and templates, and a growing sense of confidence.

Final Thoughts, Tools Serve Habits, Habits Create Skill

Tools change quickly; good habits last. The fastest path to mastering AI is not chasing every new release, but building a steady practice, saving what works, and finishing small projects. Choose a few tools, create a 20-minute routine, and protect your attention with simple rules. Over weeks and months, those small daily efforts compound into real skill, visible outputs, and the ability to earn, teach, or build with AI. You're not learning a new gadget, you're building a new capability that will support your work for years. Start small, stay consistent, and watch how quickly the tools become extensions of your creative self.

CHAPTER 8

CREATING WITH CONFIDENCE: START BEFORE YOU'RE READY

There comes a moment in every person's journey when they stand at the edge of two roads: one leads to growth, and the other leads to waiting. Most people convince themselves that they need more time, more knowledge, more courage, or more certainty before they can take the first step. They rehearse the same thoughts: *"What if I'm not good enough yet?" "What if I fail?" "What if people judge me?" "What if I embarrass myself?"* And in this quiet war between ambition and fear, perfectionism becomes the enemy disguised as protection. It tells you to wait until everything is perfect, until the timing is right, until you feel confident. But life doesn't reward hesitation, it rewards movement. And in the world of AI, where opportunities evolve daily, waiting can cost years of progress. The greatest shift you can make right now is learning to create before you feel ready, because readiness is not a starting point, it's something you build along the way.

The Trap of Perfectionism

Perfectionism is one of the most seductive mindset traps you can fall into. It hides behind noble intentions, "I just want to do it right", but what it actually does is slow you down, drain your energy, and prevent you from ever launching anything. Perfectionism makes you overthink every tiny detail of your work. It forces you to rewrite sentences that were already good, redesign an image twenty times, record and delete videos because your voice wasn't "perfect," or compare your starting point to someone else's 10th year of mastery. It makes you believe that anything less than flawless is a failure. But here's the truth: no creator, entrepreneur, or innovator has ever achieved perfection. Everything you admire, from books to businesses to videos to digital empires, began imperfectly. Some of the most successful brands in the world started with rough, flawed, and simple ideas that grew through time, feedback, and consistency. The people who rise are not the ones who wait until they're ready. They are the ones who dare to begin while shaking, uncertain, and absolutely imperfect.

AI brings a powerful gift to perfectionists: speed. Instead of spending hours trying to make something flawless, AI allows you to create drafts quickly, experiment easily, and see results faster. It gives you permission to improve later. Progress, not perfection, is what leads to growth. When you understand this, perfectionism loses its power over you.

How AI Helps You Start Faster

One of the most incredible advantages of the AI revolution is that it reduces the time between idea and execution to almost zero. In the past, if you wanted to write a blog post, you might spend days brainstorming topics, outlining content, drafting paragraphs, editing, rewriting, and formatting. Today, you can ask AI to generate a starting draft within seconds. If you want to design a social media post, build a landing page, create a video, or brainstorm business ideas, AI accelerates everything. This speed matters because momentum builds confidence. When you see your ideas turn into something real in minutes instead of months, your brain shifts from *"I don't know if I can do this"* to *"Wait... maybe I can."*

AI helps remove the emotional friction that stops most beginners. You no longer have to stare at a blank page, worry about where to start, or feel stuck in confusion. AI becomes your co-creator, a partner who helps you take the first step, who gives structure to your thoughts, who pushes you forward when hesitation tries to hold you back. The faster you produce, the faster you learn. And the faster you learn, the more confident you become.

Creating Before You Feel Confident

We often believe confidence must come before action. We tell ourselves, *"Once I'm confident, I'll start a YouTube channel," "Once I'm confident, I'll launch my digital product," "Once I'm confident, I'll start offering services,"* but confidence doesn't magically appear. Confidence is a by-product of doing. You gain confidence by trying, failing, trying again, and realizing that you can survive the discomfort. Every expert you admire started as a beginner who didn't feel prepared. They felt nervous, unsure, and insecure, but they acted anyway. And with each attempt, their confidence grew. When you take action before you feel confident, you teach your mind two powerful lessons: that fear cannot stop you and that you are capable of much more than you believed.

AI accelerates this transformation. It gives you a safe, nonjudgmental space to experiment. No one has to see your drafts unless you choose to share them. You can practice privately until you feel comfortable. You can ask AI to help you rewrite something, review your work, guide you step by step, or brainstorm ideas with you. This makes action less intimidating and more approachable. You don't have to be ready. You just have to begin.

Developing Creative Courage

Creative courage is not loud or flashy. It doesn't mean being fearless. It means being willing. Willing to try. Willing to learn. Willing to create something new even when the outcome is uncertain. Courage grows when you challenge your comfort zone. It grows when you decide that your dreams matter more than your doubts. It grows when you stop worrying about what others think and focus on who you are becoming.

AI can help you build creative courage because it reduces the risk of starting. It gives you structure, support, inspiration, and direction. It allows you to test ideas quickly and refine them without feeling overwhelmed. If you're worried about judgment, remember that every creator deals with criticism, but criticism only affects those who are not grounded in their purpose. When you understand *why* you want to create, the opinions of others lose their power. Creative courage becomes easier when you stop aiming to impress and start aiming to express.

Learning by Doing, Not Thinking

Many people stay stuck in preparation mode. They read books, watch tutorials, take courses, save motivational quotes, and study inspirational creators, but they never begin. They convince themselves that learning more will remove all fear. But no amount of studying can replace experience. You don't learn how to swim by watching others swim. You learn by stepping into the water. The same applies to AI. You cannot fully understand it, leverage it, or master it by merely researching. You must interact with it. You must type your first prompt, test your first tool, create your first piece of content, and experiment with real projects.

AI rewards doers. The more you practice, the more intuitive everything becomes. Instead of waiting to understand everything perfectly, start with what you know and let the learning unfold naturally. When you give yourself permission to be a beginner, you open the door to massive growth. And every small project you complete compounds into mastery. Action beats analysis. Execution beats planning. Doing beats thinking.

Small Wins → Big Confidence

Confidence grows through evidence. When you take small consistent actions, each one becomes proof that you are capable. These small wins matter more than you think. The first AI-generated design you create, the first article you write using AI assistance, the first video you edit, the first prompt you build, the first digital product you launch, all of these micro-achievements add up until confidence becomes your natural state. You begin to trust yourself. You begin to realize that you don't need to have everything figured out to move forward. Small wins create momentum. Momentum creates progress. And progress creates unshakable confidence.

Many of the most successful digital creators today didn't start with big victories. They started with tiny steps. Their first pieces of content were not viral. Their first projects were not perfect. Their first attempts were invisible to the world. But they kept going. They built their creative muscles one day at a time, and slowly, their small wins turned into extraordinary results. The same can happen for you.

Using AI to Stay Consistent

Consistency is the bridge between goals and results. Many people have ambition, talent, and ideas, but they lack consistency. AI gives you a major advantage here. It helps you stay organized, reminds you of your tasks, helps you create content faster, generates ideas when you feel stuck, and reduces the time required for execution. Consistency becomes easier when you're supported by a tool that removes friction. You don't need to spend hours planning. You can spend minutes creating. And with each day of consistent action, your skills improve, your creativity strengthens, and your confidence deepens.

Overcoming Fear of Being Seen

One of the most common fears among beginners is the fear of being visible. You worry that people will notice your imperfections. You worry about criticism, comparison, or rejection. But hiding your gifts serves no one, not the world, not your future self, and not the people who might be inspired by your journey. AI can help you push through this fear by giving you tools to refine and elevate your work until you feel proud of it. It helps you present yourself with professionalism even as a beginner. And once your first piece of content is out in the world, the fear begins to fade. You realize that most people are too busy living their own lives to judge yours. You realize that creation is more fulfilling than hiding. You realize that showing up is not something to fear, it's something to celebrate.

Your First Step Matters More Than You Think

Every journey you admire began with one step. Not the perfect step. Not the confident step. Just the first step. And today, you have all the tools you need to begin. You have AI as your assistant, your collaborator, your creative partner. You have ideas, ambition, curiosity, and a desire to grow. You don't need permission. You don't need perfection. You only need the courage to start.

The world is changing rapidly, and those who take action early will rise the fastest. You don't need to become an expert today. You only need to begin today. And once you do, everything else will follow.

Exercise: Publish Your First AI-Created Piece of Content

Your challenge for this chapter is simple but powerful. Today, not tomorrow, not next week, create and publish *one* piece of content using AI. It can be small. It can be simple. It can be imperfect. But it must be real, visible, and completed. For example: a social media post created with AI text, an AI-assisted blog paragraph, a short video edited using an AI tool, a digital design made with Canva AI, or a simple carousel. Choose something easy and publish it publicly. This is not about the quality of the content, it's about stepping into visibility, breaking the perfection barrier, and proving to yourself that you can create before you feel ready. Once you take this first step, your confidence will shift instantly. You will feel the momentum. And from that moment forward, you will never be the same.

CHAPTER 9

OVERCOMING FEAR, DOUBT & IMPOSTER SYNDROME

There comes a moment on every journey—especially one as powerful and life-changing as learning and earning with AI—when the biggest barrier is no longer the technology, the skills, or the opportunities. The biggest barrier becomes *you*. The doubts you carry. The fears you've collected. The memories of past failures. The voices you've internalized. The hesitation that whispers, *"Are you sure you can do this?"* Every ambitious person, at some point, faces these inner storms. The truth is fearless people don't exist. What does exist are people who learn to move forward even while fear sits in the passenger seat. This chapter is designed to help you recognize those inner blocks, understand them with compassion, and rise above them with strength. Because the person you are becoming deserves to step into the world—not quietly, not cautiously, but confidently.

"Who am I to do this?" — The Root of Imposter Syndrome

One of the most common internal questions that stops creators and entrepreneurs is: *"Who am I to do this?"* You may have felt this the first time you considered starting an AI side hustle, launching a digital product, writing content, or offering a service. You worry that you're not qualified enough, not smart enough, not experienced enough, not talented enough. But imposter syndrome does not attack the unambitious—it attacks those who dream. The moment you imagine a bigger version of yourself, insecurity tries to protect you by pulling you back into the familiar.

Imposter syndrome isn't proof that you're incapable. It's proof that you're growing. It's proof that you're stepping into something new, something meaningful, something that stretches your identity. Every expert you admire has felt this at every stage of their journey. Artists, CEOs, writers, leaders, and innovators all fight the same whisper: *"What if I'm not enough?"* The difference is they don't let the whisper stop them. They act anyway, and with each small win, their inner voice transforms from doubt into belief.

AI makes this easier, because it softens the pressure of having to "know everything." You're not alone in your work. You have a tool that guides you, supports you, fills gaps, and makes creation smoother. Instead of "Who am I to do this?" the better question becomes: *"Why NOT me?"*

The Fear of Failure — The Most Human Fear of All

Fear of failure is one of the strongest emotional forces on the planet. It has stopped more dreams than lack of talent ever has. When you fear failure, you imagine worst-case scenarios. You fear embarrassment. You fear regret. You fear losing time or money. But failure is not a final destination. It is a teacher, a guide, a badge of courage. No successful person has avoided failure; they've simply learned to use it. When you try something and it doesn't work, you learn. When you learn, you adjust. When you adjust, you improve. This cycle is what creates success.

AI helps reduce the emotional cost of failure. It lets you test ideas quickly. It helps you pivot without losing time. It allows you to learn faster and recover faster. Instead of spending months preparing and planning, you can experiment in days or even hours. This reduces the stakes, and when the stakes are lower, fear shrinks. Failure becomes a stepping stone instead of a mountain.

It's important to understand that failure only hurts when you attach your identity to the outcome. When you believe that failing at a task means *you* are a failure, everything becomes terrifying. But when you separate who you are from what you try, you liberate yourself. Failure doesn't define you—it refines you. And every attempt makes you stronger.

Fear of Looking Stupid — The Silent Killer of Creativity

If people weren't afraid of looking stupid, the world would be filled with creators, entrepreneurs, artists, and innovators. Most of the time, people don't fear the task—they fear the judgment. You worry that someone will laugh at you. Someone will roll their eyes. Someone will think your idea is silly, your skills are basic, or your attempts are embarrassing. But consider this: the people who judge are rarely the ones doing anything courageous themselves. Those who create understand the struggle. Those who innovate know the discomfort. Those who try appreciate the bravery.

AI allows you to practice, experiment, rehearse, and improve privately. You can refine your work behind the scenes until you feel proud of it. This takes away a large part of the fear because you don't have to start in public. You can build quietly, develop your skills slowly, and emerge confidently. Besides, the person who risks looking foolish today becomes the person others admire tomorrow. Every master was once clumsy. Every performer was once awkward. Every expert was once inexperienced. What matters is not how you start, but that you start.

Confidence Is Created, Not Inherited

Many people assume that confidence is something you are born with—that some people naturally have it and others don't. But confidence is not a genetic blessing. It is a muscle. It grows through repetition, action, and resilience. You create confidence by proving to yourself that you can survive discomfort. You build confidence through small wins, through daily habits, through showing up on the days you feel like hiding.

AI becomes a confidence-building partner because it gives you instant support. Instead of facing challenges alone, you have a coach who guides you, a collaborator who helps you think, and an assistant who fills gaps in your abilities. When the weight of creation is shared, the burden feels lighter. As you create more with AI, your internal belief system begins to shift. You start to think like someone capable. You begin to identify as someone who takes action. And your confidence becomes a byproduct of your consistency.

The Science of Courage — Why Fear Is Not a Stop Sign

Courage is not the absence of fear. Neuroscience shows that fear activates the amygdala, the part of the brain designed to keep you safe. The problem is that the brain confuses emotional risk with physical danger. Posting a video online feels, to your brain, like standing in front of a wild animal. Trying something new feels like stepping off a cliff. But courage is the act of telling your brain, *"I hear you… but we are doing this anyway."*

Studies show that when you face fear repeatedly, your brain builds new neural pathways that make the experience easier over time. This is why the first time you post online feels terrifying, but the tenth time feels normal. Courage is built through exposure. AI helps lower the fear threshold by simplifying the tasks that intimidate you. It guides you step-by-step through things that once felt overwhelming, helping your brain adapt more smoothly.

Courage is learned. Courage is trained. Courage grows with use.

Your New Identity: Someone Who Tries

The most powerful identity you can adopt is not "an expert," "a master," or "a leader." The most powerful identity is *someone who tries.* Someone who shows up. Someone who gives effort even when fear whispers. Someone who believes in growth more than perfection. When you see yourself as someone who tries, you win twice. First, because you act. Second, because you remove the pressure of having to be flawless.

The people who transform their lives are not the ones who know everything. They are the ones who are willing to learn everything. They try again and again, using each attempt to build experience, resilience, and self-trust. With AI by your side, trying becomes easier. You no longer step into the unknown alone.

You have a guide, a partner, a library, a strategist, and a tutor at your fingertips.

Your identity shifts the moment you stop asking, *"Can I do this?"* and start saying, *"I am someone who learns, someone who tries, someone who grows."*

Becoming Unstoppable

You become unstoppable not by avoiding fear, but by mastering it. Unstoppable people still feel doubt. They still worry, still question, still hesitate. But they have one core belief: the belief that their future is worth the discomfort. The belief that their goals deserve courage. The belief that they are capable of adaptation, growth, and reinvention.

When you combine action with AI, you create a powerful momentum machine. You create faster. You learn faster. You overcome setbacks faster. The barriers that once held you back become stepping stones. The doubts that once silenced you become background noise. You realize that you are not fragile—you are adaptable. You are not unprepared—you are learning. You are not behind—you are in the process. And this process, embraced fully, makes you unstoppable.

Fear becomes smaller with every step you take. Doubt becomes quieter with every project you complete. Imposter syndrome fades when you start seeing results. What felt impossible months ago becomes normal. And what feels challenging today will soon feel easy. Your journey is not about eliminating fear but expanding your capacity to move forward despite it. That is true strength. That is true transformation.

Exercise: Write a Letter to Your Future Self

Find a quiet space, take a deep breath, and write a letter addressed to the person you will be twelve months from now. Write about your hopes, your fears, your intentions, and your dreams. Write about the courage you are choosing today. Write about the risks you are willing to take, the growth you want to achieve, and the identity you are building. Write as if your future self is cheering for you—because they are. Seal the letter or save it somewhere meaningful. A year from now, when you read it, you will see how far you've come, how much you've overcome, and how powerful you truly are.

CHAPTER 10

DESIGNING YOUR AI-POWERED CAREER OR BUSINESS

There comes a moment in every learner's journey when the excitement of discovery begins to evolve into something bigger, a vision for the future. By this point in the book, you've gained clarity about what AI is, how it works, and how it can open doors to income, creativity, and growth. Now, the next step is determining how you want to use this power. Do you want a new career? A side hustle? A freelance life? A full business? This chapter is about moving from potential to purpose, transforming scattered skills into a solid, professional path. An AI-powered future isn't just about learning tools; it's about designing a life that aligns with your values, goals, and strengths.

Choosing Your Direction: Freelance, Job, or Business

The first step in building an AI-powered career is choosing the path that fits you best. There is no "one correct" direction; each path offers unique benefits. Freelancing gives you freedom. A traditional job gives you stability. A business gives you ownership. What matters is not what the world praises, but what aligns with your personal rhythm, your lifestyle, and the way you want to work.

Freelancing is often the fastest path to earning with AI. You can start with small tasks, content creation, design, video editing, social media management, research, or automation setup. You don't need formal training, huge experience, or an existing audience. You simply need to know how to use AI tools better than the average person and be willing to deliver results. Freelancing builds skills quickly because every project teaches you something new. It also offers flexibility, you decide when you work, how much you work, and who you work with. For many beginners, freelancing becomes the gateway to confidence and clarity.

AI-assisted jobs are becoming more common across every industry. Companies now want employees who can use AI to write reports, automate workflows, analyze data, generate creative content, or manage marketing campaigns. You don't need to be a programmer to work in AI-powered roles. You simply need to understand how to use the tools effectively. Whether you want remote work, corporate growth, or a stable paycheck, AI literacy makes you more competitive. In fact, AI skills are now valued as much as traditional computer skills were 20 years ago.

Starting a business is a deeper commitment, but an incredibly rewarding one. AI lowers the cost, reduces the workload, and speeds up execution. It allows you to operate like a team of five even when you're alone. You can build an agency, create digital products, start an online education brand, launch a social media business, or even create an AI-based service. Entrepreneurship gives you full control, your vision, your rules, your schedule. But it also requires responsibility, consistency, and courage. Many people start as freelancers and, over time, grow into business owners once they find their niche.

The key is choosing a direction that feels right for *you*, not the one that sounds the most impressive. A fulfilling career is designed, not forced.

Packaging Your Skills, Turning Abilities Into Offers

Having skills is one thing. Turning them into an offer people will pay for is another. Packaging your skills means transforming everything you know into something clear, valuable, and easy for others to understand. People don't pay for your tools; they pay for outcomes. They don't care that you use ChatGPT or Canva or Midjourney. They care that you can solve their problem, meet their need, or create something they cannot do themselves.

Start by identifying what you're good at, what you enjoy, and what people struggle with. If you love writing, AI helps you write faster, research better, and offer more polished work. If you enjoy design, AI unlocks limitless creativity. If you like solving problems, you can create automation systems that save people time. The clearer your offering, the easier it is for clients or employers to understand your value.

The best offers are simple, specific, and solution-focused. Instead of telling people, "I do AI content creation," it's more effective to say, "I create SEO-optimized content using AI that helps businesses grow faster." This clarity builds trust. People want to feel confident that you can deliver. When you present your skills in a structured way, clear service, clear benefit, clear process, you turn your abilities into something marketable.

Portfolio Building with AI, Showing, Not Telling

A portfolio is one of the most powerful assets you can create on your AI journey. It shows that you don't just talk about your skills, you can prove them. And with AI, building a portfolio is easier than ever. You don't need real clients to create sample work. You can create high-quality examples by generating mock projects. Write blog posts, design graphics, produce videos, build automation flowcharts, or create digital products, all using AI as your assistant.

Your portfolio doesn't need to be huge; it needs to be effective. A small collection of strong, clear samples communicates professionalism. Each portfolio piece should highlight the problem you solved, the process you used, and the outcome you delivered. Even if the project is fictional, your execution shows capability. This is especially powerful for beginners who worry about lack of experience. AI helps bridge that gap by making your sample work look polished and professional.

Remember, people don't hire degrees, they hire results. When your portfolio demonstrates results, you stand out instantly, regardless of whether you're a beginner.

How to Price Your Services, The Value Mindset

Learning how to price your services can feel intimidating. Many beginners worry about charging too much or too little. But pricing is not about your self-worth, it's about the value you deliver. When AI helps you create high-quality work faster, your value increases because your impact increases. Instead of asking, "How much should I charge?" ask, "What is the problem I'm solving worth to the client?"

If your work saves someone time, earns them money, or improves their business, the pricing should reflect that. You don't need to start expensive. Start at a price that feels fair and comfortable. Over time, as your confidence grows and your results improve, you increase your rates. Pricing is a journey, not a final decision.

Another powerful strategy is offering tiered packages: a basic option, a standard option, and a premium option. This gives clients flexibility while making your pricing structure look more professional. AI helps you deliver high-quality work quickly, so offering multiple packages becomes easier to manage.

What matters most is believing that your work has value. AI is a tool, but *you* are the creator, the thinker, the strategist. You bring insight, communication, creativity, and decision-making. That is what people pay for.

How to Stand Out in a Busy World

The digital world is crowded, but the truth is, most people don't stand out because they don't show up consistently. You don't need to be the loudest voice; you just need to be the most authentic, helpful, and reliable. AI helps you stand out by letting you create better content, deliver faster results, and maintain high-quality work even when you're busy or overwhelmed.

What truly makes you stand out is your unique blend of personality, style, communication, experience, and values. No AI tool can replicate the human heart behind your work. When you combine your humanity with the efficiency of AI, you create something rare, authentic work delivered with modern power. Consistency is another factor. People trust those who show up. Whether you're freelancing, job-seeking, or running a business, staying visible and reliable builds your reputation over time.

Also, don’t underestimate the power of kindness and professionalism. Many freelancers and creators lose opportunities not because of lack of talent but because of poor communication. When you deliver on time, respond politely, and maintain integrity, you naturally stand out.

Building Long-Term Career Resilience, Future-Proofing Yourself

The future will favor those who adapt, learn, and stay curious. Career resilience is about making yourself unshakeable even in times of change. AI is evolving quickly, and the best way to stay relevant is simple: keep learning. You don't need to master everything. You just need to grow a little each week. The more adaptable you are, the more valuable you become.

AI literacy is not a trend; it is the foundation of future careers. The people who embrace it now will hold the strongest positions tomorrow. But long-term resilience also means taking care of your mind, your energy, and your creativity. Burnout slows growth. Self-doubt limits opportunities. The best career plan is one that includes mental strength, emotional intelligence, and personal balance.

Your AI-powered career is not built in one day. It is built through layers: skill by skill, project by project, lesson by lesson. If you stay committed to your path, even during the quiet seasons, you will build something powerful and lasting.

Exercise: Build Your AI Portfolio Outline

Take a few minutes and outline a simple AI-powered portfolio. Include sections like:

- Your introduction
- The services you offer
- 3 to 5 sample projects
- Descriptions of how you used AI
- The value each project delivers

This outline is the first step toward building your professional identity.

CHAPTER 11

Daily AI Habits for SUCCESS

Success in any field doesn't come from a single burst of effort; it comes from consistent, intentional daily habits. AI has made skill-building faster and more efficient than ever, but without a structured daily routine, even the most powerful tools can lose their impact. The purpose of this chapter is to help you establish daily habits that create momentum, sustain growth, and turn AI learning into a lifestyle rather than a project. By the end, you will have a clear roadmap to ensure that each day moves you closer to your goals, financial, professional, and personal.

10-Minute Skill Upgrades, Small Steps, Big Results

Many people believe that learning AI requires hours of study, deep technical expertise, or complicated courses. The truth is, the most powerful growth comes from consistent, small increments of skill building. Ten minutes a day may sound trivial, but over time, it accumulates into mastery. This is the principle of compound learning. Every day you practice a prompt, explore a new feature in Midjourney, or create a simple automated workflow, you are building knowledge and confidence that compounds month after month.

The key is focused, intentional practice. For example, spend ten minutes exploring a feature of ChatGPT you haven't used before, like using advanced prompting techniques or creating structured output templates. Or use ten minutes to research a trend in AI video tools. The time is short enough to be manageable, but the impact is long-term. When you commit to daily skill upgrades, you stay ahead of the curve and build momentum that accelerates your learning exponentially.

AI allows you to learn faster, but the human habit of consistency is irreplaceable. Ten minutes a day, repeated every day, will produce more results than sporadic six-hour deep dives that leave you exhausted and inconsistent.

Daily Income-Generating Tasks, Focus on What Moves the Needle

Learning AI is exciting, but the ultimate goal for many is to translate these skills into income. This requires prioritizing daily tasks that directly impact results. Instead of spending hours on endless tutorials or unstructured experiments, identify the actions that have real-world impact: writing a blog post for a client, generating social media content, designing a graphic for a small business, or building a mini digital product. Every day, you should allocate a portion of your schedule to tasks that generate tangible value.

Start small and grow gradually. Perhaps Monday is for writing content, Tuesday for building a portfolio piece, Wednesday for client outreach, and so on. The repetition will create rhythm and focus. AI tools dramatically reduce the time needed for these tasks, so you can complete in hours what used to take days. The key is to integrate income-generating work as part of your daily routine, rather than leaving it for "someday."

Remember, small consistent actions produce compound results. One well-structured social media post a day may seem minor, but over months it builds authority, trust, and visibility. Every micro-task contributes to larger success.

The 1–1–1 Rule, One Skill, One Project, One Hour

A simple yet powerful habit for consistent growth is the 1–1–1 rule: dedicate one hour a day to learning one skill and applying it to one project. This structure ensures that you are not merely consuming information, but actively converting it into output. Learning AI is exciting, but without application, knowledge remains theoretical. By committing one focused hour daily, you create a balance between skill acquisition and practical execution.

During this hour, you could practice AI writing by creating an article for your portfolio, or experiment with AI design by producing a new graphic for a mock client. One skill focuses your energy, one project ensures you create tangible results, and one hour keeps the habit sustainable. Over time, this becomes an automatic routine. You'll notice that even when you feel busy or unmotivated, you can fit in one hour, and that hour compounds into significant expertise over weeks and months.

Tracking Growth, Seeing Progress Builds Momentum

One of the most overlooked aspects of building habits is tracking growth. If you don't measure your progress, you risk losing motivation, because human brains respond to results, not effort. Tracking can be simple: maintain a journal, log tasks completed, or use a spreadsheet to track projects, income, and skill levels. Every time you see measurable growth, you feel motivated to continue.

Tracking growth also allows you to analyze patterns. Which tasks consistently lead to income or skill improvement? Which methods produce higher-quality results? Over time, you begin to optimize your routine, focusing on what works and eliminating what doesn't. This cycle of action, tracking, and optimization is what turns beginners into high-performing AI-powered professionals.

Staying Motivated, Keeping the Fire Alive

Motivation ebbs and flows, and expecting constant inspiration is unrealistic. Instead, build habits and systems that carry you when motivation wanes. Daily AI practice becomes a ritual that doesn't rely on excitement alone. That said, there are ways to keep the fire alive: celebrate small wins, reflect on progress, and revisit your "why." Why did you start learning AI? Why do you want to earn with these skills? Reconnecting to your purpose is a powerful way to reignite energy when distractions or fatigue creep in.

Another motivational strategy is accountability. Share your goals with a friend, mentor, or online community. Regular check-ins create external accountability that reinforces internal discipline. AI also offers virtual motivation: tools like Notion AI can track progress, suggest new challenges, or remind you to practice. The combination of internal commitment and external support makes consistency much easier.

Bouncing Back After Setbacks, Resilience is Key

Even with consistent habits, setbacks are inevitable. Maybe a client project fails, a workflow doesn't produce expected results, or an AI-generated output is flawed. The crucial difference between those who succeed and those who quit is the ability to bounce back. Resilience is built by treating mistakes as learning opportunities rather than evidence of failure.

AI actually makes recovery faster. If a project goes wrong, you can quickly regenerate content, redesign, or automate a correction. The key is not to dwell on the setback but to analyze it, adjust, and continue.

When you normalize challenges as part of the process, setbacks become temporary hurdles rather than roadblocks. Daily habits are especially important during these times; maintaining your routine keeps you moving forward and prevents discouragement from stalling your growth.

Creating Your Daily Success Routine

Now it's time to put it all together. Your daily AI habits should combine skill-building, application, tracking, motivation, and resilience. A sample structure might look like this:

- **Morning (10–15 minutes):** Quick skill upgrade, practice a new feature, learn a shortcut, or explore a small new capability in your AI toolkit.
- **Midday (30–45 minutes):** Apply your skill to a project, whether for income, portfolio, or learning.

- **Afternoon/Evening (10–15 minutes):** Reflect and track progress. Note achievements, identify areas for improvement, and plan for tomorrow.

Even 60–90 minutes a day with this structure creates compound results that accumulate exponentially. The routine keeps your momentum, reinforces learning, builds your portfolio, and moves you steadily toward professional success. The most important element is consistency. Even on days when you feel tired, distracted, or unmotivated, completing a small task keeps the habit alive and prevents regression.

Exercise: Create Your Daily Success Routine

Take a sheet of paper or digital document and outline your own daily AI routine. Include:

- One skill to practice

- One project to apply it to
- A time window for daily practice
- A method to track progress
- Motivational checkpoints
- A plan for recovering from setbacks

Writing this routine down transforms it from an idea into a commitment. Treat it as sacred time each day, a period dedicated to growth, creation, and building the future you desire. Over weeks and months, you'll see the results multiply. Daily habits are the foundation of extraordinary achievement, and when paired with AI, your capacity to learn, create, and earn grows faster than ever before.

Daily habits might seem small, but they are the invisible scaffolding supporting everything else. When you establish a rhythm of learning, creating, tracking, and reflecting, you are no longer dependent on motivation alone. You become unstoppable. AI provides the tools, but your habits provide the structure. Together, they form the engine that propels you forward, faster, smarter, and more resilient than ever before. By embracing these daily practices, you turn potential into reality, curiosity into skill, and effort into tangible results.

CHAPTER 12

Your New Identity: A Confident, Future-Proof You

Congratulations!!! By reaching this stage in your journey, you have not only learned about AI and high-income skills, but you have also been reshaping the most important asset you own: yourself. Learning AI is not just about mastering tools or earning money, it's about transformation. This chapter is about stepping fully into your new identity, the confident, empowered, future-proof version of yourself who can thrive in an AI-powered world. It is a guide to solidifying the habits, mindset, and strategies that will keep you growing long after you finish this book.

Rewriting Your Story, You Are the Author

Every person carries a story about who they are, what they can do, and what they deserve. Some stories limit us: "I'm too old to learn," "I'm not technical," "I could never start my own business." But stories are not facts, they are interpretations, and they can be rewritten. Your journey with AI is the perfect moment to re-author your narrative. Instead of seeing yourself as someone left behind by technology, see yourself as someone who is learning, adapting, and creating the future.

Begin by reflecting on where you were before this journey. Perhaps fear, doubt, or self-limiting beliefs held you back. Recognize those moments, but do not dwell on them. Then, consciously rewrite your story with new truths: "I am a learner, a creator, a problem solver. I embrace technology to expand my skills. I am capable of earning, growing, and reinventing myself." Writing this new story down gives it power. Repetition, reflection, and consistent action turn words into identity. Each time you act in alignment with this new story, you reinforce it, making it your lived reality rather than just an idea.

The "I Can Learn Anything" Mindset, Your Superpower

The most successful people in the AI era are not necessarily the most naturally talented, they are the most adaptable. They embrace the mindset of, "I can learn anything I need to succeed." This is your superpower. AI tools are constantly evolving, and the skills that are valuable today may shift tomorrow. By cultivating a mindset of lifelong learning, you make yourself resilient to change and prepared for opportunity.

Believing that you can learn anything requires humility and curiosity. It also requires discipline and courage. There will always be tools, techniques, or concepts that feel complicated or intimidating at first. The key is to approach them with curiosity, break them into manageable steps, and practice consistently. Every new skill you acquire, every project you complete, reinforces the truth: you are capable of learning and mastering anything necessary to thrive. This mindset becomes your foundation for all future success.

The Future Belongs to Learners

History favors the adaptable. In the past, mastery of physical skills or memorization of knowledge might have been enough. Today, the future belongs to those who are comfortable learning continuously, especially in a rapidly changing digital world. AI is a tool that accelerates learning, but it cannot replace the human capacity for curiosity, creativity, and persistence.

Your advantage lies not in perfection, but in your commitment to grow. When others hesitate, stuck in fear or waiting for "perfect" conditions, you move forward. You practice, experiment, and refine. You are not competing with tools or machines, you are competing with yourself, your previous limitations, and your unwillingness to try. Each day you learn something new, you expand your edge. By adopting a mindset of continuous growth, you ensure that you are not only ready for the future, you are shaping it.

You Now Have the Skills, Keep Going

By now, you have accumulated a toolkit of AI skills, productivity habits, and entrepreneurial knowledge. You know how to create, automate, and monetize. But skills alone are not enough; action is what turns knowledge into results. Keep going. Keep building, refining, and testing your abilities. Every project, no matter how small, reinforces your confidence and your credibility.

Many beginners make the mistake of pausing once they feel "ready." True mastery, however, comes from persistent application. Apply your skills to real-world problems, whether for clients, your own projects, or community initiatives. Each attempt, success, and even failure reinforces your identity as someone who acts, creates, and delivers. Remember: the goal is progress, not perfection. Forward motion, no matter the pace, creates momentum and builds a track record of success.

Your Next 90 Days, A Transformational Sprint

Now is the time to set a concrete plan. The next 90 days are a powerful period for transformation. This is not about vague resolutions, it's about intentional, structured action. Think of this as your sprint toward a more confident, capable, and future-proof self. Set specific goals that cover skills, projects, and outcomes. For example, you might commit to mastering one new AI tool, completing three portfolio projects, and generating your first $500 using your skills.

Structure your plan with daily habits in mind: allocate time for skill development, practical application, and reflection. Review progress weekly, adjust goals if needed, and celebrate wins, both big and small. By the end of 90 days, the cumulative impact of consistent effort will transform your skills, mindset, and confidence. You will no longer see yourself as someone who "wants" to succeed, you will see yourself as someone who *does* succeed.

The Gift of Reinvention, Embrace Your New Identity

One of the most powerful lessons of this journey is that you are not fixed. Reinvention is your right and your responsibility. Every time you learn, apply, and adapt, you shed limitations and embrace potential. AI accelerates this process, but the true gift comes from within: the willingness to step into a new version of yourself.

Reinvention is not just professional; it is personal. As you develop competence, confidence, and clarity, you naturally begin to embody the qualities of someone capable, resilient, and creative. You take on challenges with curiosity rather than fear. You see opportunity rather than obstacle. This is the essence of a future-proof identity, someone who thrives in change, harnesses technology, and continues to grow without fear of the unknown.

Exercise: Your 90-Day Transformation Plan

To solidify your new identity, create a detailed 90-day plan. Start by identifying three main focus areas: one skill to master, one income-generating project, and one personal habit to reinforce confidence or productivity. Break these into weekly tasks. For each week, identify the action steps, deadlines, and measurable outcomes.

Next, incorporate reflection points. Every Sunday, review your progress, adjust strategies, and note lessons learned. Celebrate achievements, analyze setbacks, and recommit to the next week. By the end of the 90 days, you will have tangible results, new skills, completed projects, and a reinforced sense of capability. More importantly, you will have transformed your identity into someone who acts, learns, earns, and thrives.

Stepping Into Your Future, A Final Word

As you close this chapter and this book, remember that your journey is only beginning. Learning AI and building high-income skills are not endpoints, they are lifelong tools for growth. Your new identity is now rooted in confidence, capability, and resilience. You have learned how to acquire skills, take action, overcome fear, and adapt to change. You have practiced daily habits, built a portfolio, and started generating value.

The future belongs to learners like you, those who embrace technology, take action, and refuse to be limited by past beliefs or current circumstances. Keep building, keep experimenting, and keep showing up. Reinvent yourself as often as necessary, but always maintain the core belief: you are capable of learning anything, creating impact, and thriving in a world of constant change.

Your transformation is complete, not because the learning stops, but because your mindset, identity, and habits have been rewritten. You are now someone who faces the future with confidence, adaptability, and courage. Every day forward is an opportunity to expand, create, and earn. The tools, skills, and mindset are yours. Your future is yours to design. Step into it boldly.

FINAL CHAPTER

THE AI SUCCESS ROADMAP: YOUR COMPLETE GUIDE TO MOVING FORWARD

The journey you've taken through this book has helped you learn new skills, transform how you see yourself, overcome fear, unlock confidence, and step into the world of AI with courage. Now, this final chapter is your long-term guide — a roadmap you can follow for the rest of your life.

Most people learn something powerful… then do nothing with it. Not because they're lazy, but because they don't have a system. Transformation is not built on motivation; it is built on structure, habits, clarity, and repetition.

This chapter gives you exactly that.

You'll walk away with:

- A 12-month AI success plan
- A weekly and monthly structure
- Tables to help you track skills, income goals, and progress
- Decision frameworks
- A professional growth blueprint
- A resilience plan for when life gets hard
- A personal "AI Mastery Dashboard"
- And your lifelong learning system

Let's begin designing your future.

SECTION 1 — The 3 Pillars of Lifelong AI Mastery

Every successful AI learner and earner builds their life around three pillars. These pillars keep you growing even when life becomes busy, stressful, or uncertain.

Pillar 1: Continuous Learning

AI is always evolving — and so should you.

What to study continuously:

- New AI tools
- Prompt-writing techniques
- Industry trends
- Skills connected to your niche
- Case studies from successful creators

Pillar 2: Continuous Creating

Skills only grow when you use them. Every project you complete shapes your identity and builds your portfolio.

Create weekly:

- Content
- Digital products
- Tutorials / guides
- AI-powered services
- Mini-projects to sharpen your skills

Pillar 3: Continuous Earning

Whether small or big, consistent income proves that your skills have value.

Focus on earning through:

- Freelance gigs
- Selling digital products
- Subscription-based services
- Content monetization

- Helping businesses with A

SECTION 2

Your AI Success Roadmap (12-Month Plan)

Use this as your year-long guide.

📅 Table 1: Your 12-Month AI Progress Path

Month	Focus Area	What You Should Create	Expected Outcome
1	Skill Foundation	Practice prompts + micro-projects	Clear understanding of your AI niche

Month	Focus Area	What You Should Create	Expected Outcome
2	Confidence Building	Publish small work (posts, videos, samples)	Overcome fear and start showing up
3	Skill Expansion	Learn 1–2 advanced tools	Build deeper skills
4	Portfolio Creation	Create your public portfolio	Begin attracting clients
5	First Earnings	Start small freelance tasks	\$50–\$300 income
6	Product Launch	Create and sell your first digital product	Your first scalable income
7	Consistency Cycle	Weekly content + 1 product	Build momentum

AI Skills

Month	Focus Area	What You Should Create	Expected Outcome
8	Automation	Use AI to automate repetitive work	More free time
9	Higher-Value Skills	Learn business-focused AI use cases	Ability to charge more
10	Personal Brand	Build online presence professionally	Become visible in your niche
11	Income Scaling	Add new products/services	Higher monthly earnings
12	Mastery & Review	Assess skills, update goals	Enter new year stronger

SECTION 3

The Weekly and Daily System

If your system is strong, your success becomes automatic.

Daily Routine (The 1–1–1 AI Rule)

Every day:

1 Skill practiced (10–20 min)

1 Project updated or created (20–40 min)

1 Hour of deep work (pure focus time)

Even if you're busy, this keeps you growing.

SECTION 4

Your AI Skill Tracker

📋 Table 2: Skill Tracking Dashboard

Skill	Current Level	Goal Level	Tools to Use	Deadline
Prompt Writing	Beginner	Advanced	ChatGPT, Gemini	30 days
Graphic Design	Beginner	Intermediate	Canva, Midjourney	90 days
Automation	No Knowledge	Intermediate	Make.com, Zapier	6 months
Content Creation	Intermediate	Expert	ChatGPT, CapCut	3 months

Skill	Current Level	Goal Level	Tools to Use	Deadline
Business Skills	Beginner	Intermediate	Free online courses	6 months

SECTION 5

Your AI Income Blueprint

There are only **five** ways to make money with AI. Choose 1–2 to start.

The 5 Income Paths

Freelancing

- social media management
- copywriting
- design
- automation setups

Digital Products

- eBooks

- templates
- checklists
- prompts packs

AI-Assisted Content Creation

- YouTub
- TikTok
- blogging
- email newsletters

AI Services for Businesses

- workflow automation
- customer service chatbots
- marketing systems

Teaching / Coaching

AI Skills

- courses
- online workshops
- community memberships

📌 Table 3: Income Planning Table

Income Stream	Skill Needed	Time Required	Difficulty	Monthly Earning Potential
Freelancing	Medium	Low	Medium	$300–$1500
Digital Products	Medium	Medium	Medium	$500–$5000
Content Creation	Low	High	High	$0–$20,000
AI Services	High	Medium	High	$1,000–$10,000

Income Stream	Skill Needed	Time Required	Difficulty	Monthly Earning Potential
Coaching	High	High	High	$500–$8,000

SECTION 6

The Fear & Setback Recovery System

Life happens. Motivation drops. Projects fail. Doubts return.

Here is your recovery map.

If you feel lost → Follow the GPS Method

G — Ground yourself

Pause. Breathe. Recognize the feeling.

P — Pinpoint the block

Write down exactly what is bothering you.

S — Simplify the next step

Take ONE small action in the next 10 minutes.

If you lose motivation → use the Restart Formula

Watch 1 tutorial

Do 1 small task

Create 1 micro-win

Your brain needs momentum, not motivation.

If you face fear → The "What's the Worst?" Exercise

Ask:

- What's the worst that could realistically happen?
- What's the best that could happen?
- What's the most likely outcome?

Fear becomes smaller when your mind sees logic.

SECTION 7

Your Personal AI Mastery Dashboard

Create a dashboard you check weekly.

Table 4: AI Mastery Dashboard Template

Category	Score (1–5)	Notes	Next Step
Skills			
Confidence			
Consistency			
Creativity			
Income			
Growth Mindset			

SECTION 8

Your Reinvention Plan (90-Day Challenge)

This 90-day transformation system ensures you grow faster than ever.

The 90-Day Structure

Month 1 — Learn

Choose 1–2 AI tools and master them.

Month 2 — Build

Create your portfolio + 1 digital product.

Month 3 — Monetize

Launch, promote, and sell your work.

Use this table:

Table 5: 90-Day Transformation Planner

Day Range	Goal	What You Do
1–10	Skill foundation	Tutorials, practice prompts
11–20	Micro-projects	Create small samples
21–30	Build confidence	Publish simple work
31–40	New skill	Learn advanced features
41–50	Portfolio	Assemble your best work
51–60	Build product	Create & test
61–75	Launch	Start selling
76–90	Scaling	Improve & expand

SECTION 9

Becoming Future-Proof

AI will keep evolving. But you will not be left behind, because you know how to adapt.

The future belongs to those who:

- stay curious
- practice constantly
- experiment without fear
- embrace new tools
- reinvent themselves
- learn openly
- stay consistent

You are now one of those people.

SECTION 10

Your Final Commitment

Write this somewhere visible:

"I am not here to be perfect.

"I am here to learn, grow, and rise."

This is your identity now.

You are someone who tries.

Someone who learns.

Someone who adapts.

Someone who builds their future with courage.

Someone who uses AI not as a shortcut, but as a superpower.

Your journey begins now — and you are ready.

www.ingramcontent.com/pod-product-compliance
Lightning Source LLC
LaVergne TN
LVHW050934210926
848482LV00013B/609
* 9 7 8 1 9 1 9 5 6 0 9 0 8 *